MENUS FOR GOURMETS

MENUS FOR GOURMETS

by

ANDRÉ L. SIMON

Hearthside Press, Incorporated

Publishers ● New York

CONTENTS

MENUS FOR GOURMETS

FOREWORD

GOURMETS are all of us who happen to be born with a palate, just as singers are born with a voice. It is a gift. You cannot buy a palate any more than a voice over the counter; if it is not there, forget about it and think of something else; but if it is there you had better do something about it, for a palate, again like a voice, can be and should be trained and used. Gourmets may be rich or poor, young or old, generous or mean, greedy or not, but whether they are content with a little or want a lot, they will always do their best to get whatever is best, not necessarily what costs much, but that which looks good, smells good and tastes good both to eat and to drink. Good food and good wine are the best of partners: food never tastes better than when matched with the right wine, and most wines are also better with the right food than by themselves. There is a very great variety of foods for us to choose from and there is practically no limit to the number of different ways and means of cooking or preparing all manner of different foods. The number of wines which are available to most of us in the ordinary way of commerce is limited, but even then it is considerable and fully sufficient to make it possible for us to try different wines with different dishes according to our personal means and fancies. There are many wines which cost less than a dollar, and a bottle of wine can serve six not too thirsty gourmets: other wines of course, cost much more, and they are worth it provided, of course, that you can tell silk from cotton or appreciate, hence enjoy, the bouquet, breed and charm of a great wine of ripe age; those are qualities which are missing in younger and 'ordinaires' wines, but if you are no gourmet, you will not miss them, and there is no sense in your paying the higher price which aristocrats among wines are bound to cost.

To choose both fare and wines for our daily meals is a matter of individual taste, as well as of circumstances: the weather, the occasion, the guests and the mood of the moment all have to do with our choice. Which is why a book of Menus can never be anything better than an expression of personal opinion. The thirty Menus in this little book are merely those of fifteen Luncheons and fifteen dinners which I would enjoy at different seasons of the year and on different occasions, festive or otherwise. They will not appeal to all gourmets in all parts of the world—no set of Menus can ever do so, but they may—and I trust that they will be a guide which will help many gourmets make up their own Menus with greater originality and more perfect balance.

French names have been given to French dishes for the simple reason that a dish is just as much entitled to keep its name as any one of us. When Monsieur Jean Lebrun comes to the United States, he does not become John Brown Esquire, any more than Miss Green would be dubbed Mademoiselle Epinard if she went to Paris. But, besides the unfairness of robbing a dish of its own name, it does not help anybody. Gourmets who have had a *Sole Meuniere* before, know, when they see the name on a Menu, what to expect: those who have never had it before or have had it but do not remember what it was, will not be any the wiser if they see on the Menu *Sole of the miller's wife;* or if they see *Mussels of the mariner's daughter* instead of *Moules Mariniere.* Whether any miller ever had a wife who put a pat of butter in the middle of a fried sole; or whether any mariner ever had a daughter who cooked mussels in white wine, nobody knows and nobody cares, *Meuniere* and *Mariniere* happen to be the names given by some French cook to those two methods of cooking and that is all there is to it. Of course, it is just foolish to translate English names into French. A Grouse, for instance, is always a Grouse and not *Coq de Bruyere*, as often seen on luxury hotel menus; there is no French name for a Grouse, and a *Coq de Bruyere* is *Black Game.* There is in the U.S.A. a grass seed which is called *Wild Rice* and is very good but not in the least like rice. Its name on Menus should always be *Wild Rice* and never *Riz sauvage.*

Hors d'oeuvre is the opening course of a meal, and so is soup, but no meal requires both openings, and, personally, I like *Hors d'oeuvre* for lunch, and no soup, but Soup for dinner, and no Hors d'oeuvre. There are many, however, who like both at the same meal, and there is no reason why they should not have what they like.

QUANTITIES

Throughout the book the quantities given in the recipes are for serving from four to six persons.

SALADS AND SALAD DRESSINGS

In most, if not actually all our Luncheon Menus there is a designedly vague mention of "Salad." There are two reasons for this: the first is my own belief that some fresh, uncooked, dressed or undressed salad should be part of all good luncheons, simple or otherwise. The second is that it is best to be vague and let the choice of the salad to be served rest with the taste of the host or hostess and whatever they may be able to get locally at different times of the year.

Some guidance as to the choice of a salad may however, prove to be of use, hence the following notes.

By far the most popular of all salads is the *Lettuce,* the generic name of a variety of salads, chiefly the following: (a) *Cabbage Lettuce.* Lat. *Lactuca sativa, var. Capitata;* Fr. *Laitue;* (b) *Romaine or Cos Lettuce.* Lat. *Lactuca sativa, var. Longifolia;* Fr. *Romaine;* (c) *Small* or *Cutting Lettuce;* this is a lettuce which never forms a head, but produces leaves almost continuously during the summer months; it is valuable where space is limited, as it does not run to seed, and it provides a green salad so long as its leaves are cut off regularly; (d) *Perennial Lettuce.* This is an uncultivated lettuce with leaves not unlike those of the *Dandelion.* It grows freely in light and chalky soils in many parts of France, and its young leaves are very much appreciated in the spring of the year for salads.

The first and foremost place for all kinds of lettuce is in the salad bowl. The lettuce should be washed very carefully in plenty of cold, salted water, which is easy; then it should be thoroughly well dried, which is not so easy. The best way is to put the lettuce into a wire basket and either swing it or rotate it until all the water is forced out. Failing a wire basket, the wet lettuce can also be swung in a piece of thin muslin, but it must *not* be *pressed,* not even patted, otherwise the salad will be lifeless and lose the crispness which is its chief gastronomical asset. Freshly picked, crisp, young cos or Romaine lettuce is most acceptable with just a grain of salt, undressed, with bread and cheese. But, of course, any lettuce served as a salad course should be dressed; the usual dressing consists of two parts of olive oil to one of wine-vinegar or lemon juice, and two of salt to one of pepper, with variations according to individual tastes. That sort of dressing, however, is merely the beginning or under garments; a salad, to be properly dressed, should also be given the added flavor of finely chopped *Fines Herbes,* that is, tarragon, chervil and the green tops of chives or spring onions; there are other herbs which may be introduced by the way of a change from time to time.

The Chicory and the Endive come next to the Lettuce in popular favor. Lat. *Chicorium Intybus;* Fr. *Endive; Chicorée sauvage; Barbe de Capucin.* A European weed which had been used in its natural or wild form as well as when improved by cultivation, both as food and medicine, during many centuries. The roots of the wild chicory are long and thin, like over-grown radishes; they are lifted and planted in the autumn in moderately heated houses and in complete darkness; they produce long, thin, bitter leaves, silvery white at the base and pale yellow at the tip; they are used as a salad, popular in France under the name of *Barbe de Capucin.* An improved variety which is popular in Switzerland under the name of *Salade des Alpes,* is known to seedsmen by the name of *Chicorée de Trevise* or *Treviso.* Its tips are pale mauve and harmonize excellently with the deeper mauve of cooked beetroot.

The largest and best variety of cultivated chicory is known as *Chicory Witloof* or *Endive de Bruxelles;* its roots are like small parsnips and its tightly-packed silvery leaves are eaten either uncooked as a salad, or cooked in many different ways as a vegetable.

A closely related species, known as *Magdeburg Chicory,* is not suitable for forcing; it is grown chiefly for the sake of its roots, which are as large as those of the *Witloof* and are used, roasted and ground, to adulterate coffee.

ENDIVE. Lat. *Chichorium endiva;* Fr. *Chicorée frisée.* One of the finest of salads, it is a native of the East. There are many varieties of endive, all of them derived from *Cichorium pumilum,* the wild Mediterranean endive. When not otherwise qualified, endive means one or other of the curled-leaved varieties, such as the *Anjou,* or small green curled summer endive; the *Meaux,* or small green fine curled winter endive; the *Picpus,* or curled endive; the *Stag's Horn,* or *Rouen* endive; the *Louviers* or *Ruffec* moss-curled endive; the ever-white curled endive, etc. All broad-leaved varieties are called *Batavian Endive.*

A slate or tile placed in the center of an endive, when almost fully grown, is all that is necessary to bleach its "heart" or "head," which is thereby rendered not only white or paler yellow, but more tender, hence more suitable for eating uncooked as a salad.

In the U.S.A. endive is known as chicory, and is sometimes called *French Endive.* There is also a green salad known as *Green Endive,* which is neither endive nor chicory, but the *Prickly Lettuce.*

A winter and early spring salad which is very highly appreciated in France but not nearly so much in the U.S.A. is the Corn Salad, also called Lamb's Lettuce, although it is not related to the Lettuce. Its Latin name is *Valerianella olitoria;* and its French name is *Mâche* or *Doucette.* It is a European weed which has been improved greatly by long years of cultivation and has become one of the most popular winter salads in France and Italy. The more extensively grown varieties are the French, or round-leaved corn salad, so called in opposition to the Italian corn salad (Lat. *V. eriocarpa*), the leaves of which are lighter in color, longer and somewhat toothed on the edges. Corn salad should be picked when the leaves are still quite small. It is one of the few green salads dressed without chopped herbs; it is usually served with thin slices of cooked, red beet; also with both cooked beets and thin sticks of uncooked celery; when dressed thus, its French culinary name is *Salade Lorette.*

[Editorial note: Corn salad is easily cultivated in this country. It may be planted from seed which many of the seed catalogs list.]

Last and least of the green salads we place the garden cress, winter cress and watercress; also purslane and turnip tops or greens.

CRESS. GARDEN CRESS. Lat. *Lepidium sativum;* Fr. *Cresson aliénois.* A native of Persia which can be grown quickly and easily almost anywhere. Its tiny leaves are used for garnishing and the fillings of sandwiches. Quite a different plant from *Watercress.* Lat. *Nasturtium officinale;* Fr. *Cresson de fontaine.* An aquatic plant, a native of Europe, which grows freely in moist meadows and close to the banks of many streams. It is largely cultivated by market gardens near all large cities and it is used for garnishing or decorating dishes as well as in salads. There is another European species of watercress, the meadow cress, which bears attractive clusters of pale mauve flowers in the early spring, but its leaves have no gastronomic merit whatever.

All these green salads may be and are really best served by themselves. Radishes, tomatoes, cucumber and the like are very often added to green salads in the United States and England, but their inclusion in the green salad bowl is sheer heresy; they are much better served separately, as hors d'oeuvre, the radishes by themselves, the tomatoes in a more vinegary than oily dressing, and the shaved cucumber with a dressing more oily than vinegary.

The average middle-class household salad is an abomination, consisting of wet lettuce cut up small with a steel knife, and uncored halves of tomatoes, mostly ruined by some bottled "dressing," in the manufacture of which pure olive oil is never used.

The best all-round Salad Dressing is the *Vinaigrette* which is simply three parts of good olive oil to one part of wine-vinegar, salt and pepper thoroughly well mixed together. Chopped chervil, tarragon, chives, capers and gherkins are optional and welcome additions.

LUNCHEONS

MENU I

Hors d'oeuvre

Sardines in oil; filleted anchovies in oil; sliced uncooked tomatoes and cooked little leeks in an oil and vinegar dressing.

Oeufs au fromage

*   *   *

Navarin aux Pommes

*   *   *

Romaine or Cos Lettuce

*   *   *

Apple Rings

A simple meal, and quite a good meal, which demands simple wines, simple but good, such as a young Sylvaner of Alsace, nicely chilled but not frozen, with the Hors d'oeuvre and the eggs; it could be followed by an equally young but genuine Beaujolais. Beaujolais has become so popular that the demand now is much greater than the supply and all kinds of red wines are dubbed Beaujolais which are not even French wines: most real Beaujolais are sold under the name of their native village or vineyard—Brouilly, Fleurie, St. Amour, etc. To finish with, a glass of ruby or tawny Port would be most acceptable.

RECIPES

Oeufs au Fromage

A large, shallow baking pan, is best for this dish: butter it well, then put in it the required number of thinly cut rounds of bread which you will have dipped in oiled butter first. Upon each round of bread place a wafer of Swiss cheese of the same size, then put the dish under a hot grill or into a hot oven for as long as may be necessary for the cheese to melt and soak into the bread, but not long enough for it to brown. Remove the pan, and quickly but carefully break an egg upon each piece of cheesed bread. Sprinkle over a little salt and pepper, and a dusting of grated Swiss cheese: color gently under the grill or in the oven, and serve hot.

Navarin aux Pommes

This may be called the French *edition de luxe* of the homely Irish Stew. Most important of all is to choose the right kind of meat, cutlets or the meaty part of a shoulder of lamb: trim off most of the fat, and season the meat with salt and pepper, and well as a pinch of brown sugar if you happen to be in an adventurous disposition. Put ¼ cup of butter in a heavy iron pot or pan, and as soon as it is sizzling hot put in the meat which you will have cut into pieces of about the same size; toss them in the hot fat to brown them, and then add about ½ lb. of sliced onion which should be cooked to a golden brown, being stirred about all the time. Now is the time to sprinkle into the pot several tablespoons of flour, stirring steadily to make sure that every piece of meat shall be coated with flour. Then add stock or water just enough to cover the meat and onion, season with pepper and salt, also a crushed clove of garlic, put the lid on pan and let all cook gently for an hour. It will then be time to add small, whole new potatoes which look better than large ones cut up in pieces; cover again the pan tightly and keep it on a slow fire as long as may be necessary for the potatoes to be well cooked; by then the meat should be tender and tasty, and all that remains to be done is to skim off any excess of fat, and to serve the *Navarin aux Pommes* piping hot.

Apple Rings

Peel and core some large, acid cooking apples and slice them up horizontally in ½ in. thick rounds or "rings.' Melt a spoonful of butter in a frying pan and add twice as much sugar; mix well, then put in the apple "rings" as soon as the butter will begin to smoke—and before it gets brown. Cook the apple rings in the hot caramel mixture, first one side and then the other until both are golden: serve hot.

MENU II

Pâté de Porc en Terrine

*   *   *

Raie au Beurre noir

*   *   *

Veau Marengo

*   *   *

Apple Tart

A more elaborate meal than the last, hence an occasion for rather more distinguished wines. As there is no red meat, and as there are many people who prefer white to red wines in the morning, two white German wines should prove very enjoyable with this Menu. The first might be a young, fragrant, flowery Saar wine, such as a *Wiltinger Kupp,* served with both the Hors d'oeuvre and the fish course: it would lead the way admirably to a fuller, richer, and if possible also an older Hock, one of the better wines of the Rüdesheim Berg, for instance. Both white wines should be served cold, of course, but not iced: a wine which is too cold does not only lose most of its flavor, but it numbs the taste buds to such an extent that there is no taste left to anything.

RECIPES

Pâté de Porc en Terrine

(For a *Pâté* of 1½ pounds.) Remove skin and sinews from ½ pound of fresh pork meat, ½ pound fresh veal and 4 ounces lean beef; chop very finely and season with a good deal of salt and pepper as well as any cottage herbs that you may be able to get. Line a *Terrine* with fresh pork fat, and then half fill it with the mixed, chopped meats, pressing them well down evenly: cover this with rashers of pork fat and then add the rest of the mixed chopped meats. Now forget economy and pour over it all a glassful of Brandy not the finest Cognac that money will buy, of course, but good Cognac brandy all the same: it will make all the difference to the Pâté presently. Cover the Terrine and cook the Pâté in a moderate oven for an hour; remove lid and continue to cook until the tip of a sharp knife may be driven easily to the bottom of the Terrine and come out quite clean. Then place a round of buttered paper and a board on top of the Pâté, put on a weight that will press everything down evenly, let it get quite cold and you will then be able to cut and serve thin slices from the Terrine.

Raie au Beurre Noir

First things must always be first and in this case the first thing to do is to make a good *Court-bouillon*. And this is the way to make a right *Court-bouillon*. Put, say, one pint of water and one of white wine to boil; add a tablespoonful of vinegar; one or two (according to size) cut-up onions; one or two carrots; one clove of garlic; a small stick of celery; one or two shallots; pepper and salt, and, last but not least, the usual "bouquet garni" (parsley, thyme and a bay leaf). Let all this simmer gently for an hour, and then put the skate in it and let it cook in it, allowing 15 minutes per pound weight of fish. When the fish is done, take it out carefully to avoid breaking it and keep hot. Brown some butter until almost but not quite black. Remove pan from the fire and put in it a tablespoonful of good vinegar. Pour this butter-cum-vinegar kind of gravy over the fish and serve hot. Sprigs of fried parsley help to decorate this dish, and whole or chopped capers may also be added at the last moment.

Veau Marengo

3 tablespoons olive oil
2 pounds breast of veal
½ pound onion, chopped
2 tablespoons flour
1 cup dry white wine
2 cups bouillon (stock)
½ pound sliced mushrooms
1 pound ripe tomatoes
Salt and Pepper

Heat the olive oil and brown it in the cut up meat, then add the chopped onion, browning also a little with meat. Sprinkle with flour, browning that also, then moisten with the mixed wine and bouillon or stock. Season well. Add the sliced mushrooms and the tomatoes, previously reduced to a pulp by slow cooking after peeling. Cover pan closely and allow contents to simmer gently for at least an hour and a half.

Apple Tart

Peel and core 1½ pounds of acid cooking apples; dice them and put them in a pan with from ½ to ¾ cup of sugar, according to taste, and from 4 to 6 pats of fresh butter. Cover the pan and stew on a low heat for 15 minutes; then remove from the fire and let the apples get cold.

Prepare ½ pound rough puff pastry and line a pastry tin with it; fill with the cold and partly stewed apples; brush over with sugar, glaze and bake for 20 minutes. Serve when cold and with fresh cream.

MENU III

Hors d'oeuvre: marinated Herrings and
Potato Salad

*   *   *

Scrambled eggs with Chicken livers

*   *   *

Braised Beef and grilled Mushrooms

*   *   *

Sea-kale Salad

*   *   *

Cheese Board

*   *   *

Coffee

With the Hors d'oeuvre and the eggs, one of the less expensive white wines will be more suitable than one of the great aristocrats: a young and fresh Muscadet from the Loire, for instance. But the Beef and grilled Mushrooms should be partnered with a really fine wine, a Claret, for instance, either from the Médoc, like Château Cantemerle; or the Graves de Bordeaux, like a Domaine de Chevalier; or a Pomerol, like Château Petrus. With the cheese and the salad, which may be served separately or at the same time, a glass, and maybe two, of a light Tawny Port would be rather nice.

RECIPES

Marinated Herrings

Clean, wipe and split the fish, remove backbone and season well with salt and pepper. Cover with chopped onion and pieces of bay leaf. Roll the two halves of the fish neatly and tightly and place them in an earthenware jar; fill the jar with the best red wine vinegar available and water in equal parts. Cover the top of the jar with greaseproof paper safely tied; put the jar in a moderate oven and bake for an hour and a quarter. Let the fish get cold and pour over it a little more wine vinegar before serving.

Potato Salad

Boil some yellow-flesh potatoes if you can possibly get some: they are firmer, when cooked, than the white, mealy sorts. Let them get quite cold and then either slice them, if small, or dice them, if large. Pour over them a good Vinaigrette Sauce, (page 34), mix well and allow the potatoes to marinate in the vinaigrette at least an hour before the meal. Finely chopped parsley chives, and, if in season, celery, should be sprinkled over the Salad before serving.

Braised Beef

2 or 3 carrots
1 or 2 small turnips
12 to 15 small onions
1 stalk celery
1 or 2 leeks
4 or 5 pounds fresh brisket of beef
Salt and pepper
Bouquet garni
3 tablespoons butter
3 tablespoons flour

Prepare the carrots and turnips as a garnish, dicing them and putting them aside with the little onions duly peeled.

Shred the rest of the vegetables and put them at the bottom of a heavy iron pan. Lay the meat on this 'bed'; add salt and pepper, the bouquet garni and sufficient water (unless you have stock which is, of course, much better than water) barely to cover the meat. Cover pan closely and cook *very* gently for about 4 hours. Then add the prepared onions, carrots and turnips, and continue cooking until they are done. Heat the butter in a small pan, add the flour, stirring and cooking until the mixture becomes a brown 'roux,' then moisten with stock from the stewpan and strain into the larger pan, cooking until gravy is thickened. Serve hot with the vegetables as a garnish.

Scrambled Eggs with Chicken Livers

Lightly fry some chicken livers, cut them up and season them with salt and pepper and a squeeze of lemon; mix them up with the beaten egg and scramble the lot together.

Grilled Mushrooms

Choose some rather large mushrooms, wash them, and peel them; cut off the stalks to within one-half inch of caps. Let them stand for an hour in warm, melted butter, turning over from time to time; season with salt and pepper. Then cook over or under a fierce heat, turning once only.

Sea-kale Salad

The curly, crinkly, blue-green tops of sea-kale, not of the forced but of the open air variety, make an excellent salad, dressed with oil and vinegar; they are tasty and nutty; they are improved when served with finely chopped chives and tarragon leaves.

MENU IV

Oysters on the Half Shell

*　　*　　*

Broiled Smelts

*　　*　　*

Small Chickens à la Diable

*　　*　　*

Lettuce salad

*　　*　　*

Cheese Board

*　　*　　*

Coffee

Two white wines would probably be best with this Luncheon, the first might well be a Pouilly-Fuissé to partner the oysters as well as the smelts. Pouilly-Fuissé is the name of the white wines of the twin villages bearing those two names, in Burgundy, but all their better wines also bear the additional names of their native vineyard, such as Le Clos, probably the best of them.

The second white wine had better be another Burgundy, but a wine with greater breed and more body, such as a Corton-Charlemagne, for instance.

RECIPES

Broiled Smelts

Remove the backbone of 3 pounds of smelts and sprinkle the insides with pepper and salt. Beat 2 eggs, dilute with ½ cup milk, 2 tablespoons of good olive oil, and a pinch of salt. Dip the fish in flour, then in the egg mixture, and, last, in fine breadcrumbs. Then run the smelts under the broiler for 2 minutes on one side, and another 2 minutes on the other side, then run them onto the hot serving plates, then top each fish with a dab of *Maitre d'Hôtel Butter.*

Petits Poulets

(Small chickens) à la Diable. Split the chickens down the back; clean the inside well and spread all over with freshly made fairly liquid mustard; then dip in breadcrumbs and melted butter, and broil over a clear fire, or grill in the grilling pan of a gas stove. Serve with Sauce Tartare.

Sauce Tartare

Chop finely some parsley and tarragon leaves, and not quite so finely some chervil, shallots and gherkins. Then make a Mayonnaise sauce in the usual way, steadily mixing dripping olive oil and a yolk of egg, and add to it the chopped herbs as well as a little mustard when the Mayonnaise is quite stiff; add also a little vinegar and a little dry white wine to thin the sauce to the right consistency.

MENU V

Dressed Crab

*   *   *

Green eggs

*   *   *

Foie de Veau en Brochettes, Savory Potatoes and
Grilled Tomatoes

*   *   *

Apple Fool

*   *   *

Coffee

A chilled Orvieto secco, a dry Italian white wine, should prove a pleasant match for both the Crab and the Eggs, whilst a red Chianti from a reputable shipper could follow and be served with the Foie de Veau, finishing with a glass of the sweet white wine of Orvieto, the Orvieto Abbocato with the Apple Fool.

RECIPES

Dressed Crab

Twist off the claws, both large and small, then remove the flaps, and separate the upper from the lower shell or carapace. Remove the intestines and the stomach, which is a small bag near the head. Pick out carefully all pieces of meat from both body and claws, chop it finely and mix with a little well seasoned Sauce Vinaigrette (page 34). Wash and then dry the large shell and fill it with the prepared mixture. Decorate with some of pieces of the small claws and chopped parsley. Be careful not to leave any small bits of shell in the crab meat.

Sauce Vinaigrette

Mix together 3 parts of wine vinegar and 1 part of olive oil, salt, pepper, chopped capers, gherkins, parsley, chervil and tarragon leaves.

Green Eggs

Cooked spinach
Butter
Minced parsley
1 or 2 finely chopped mushrooms
Fried croûtons
White sauce
Salt and pepper
Onion juice
Eggs
Slices of ham

Having cooked and chopped or sieved the spinach, nicely seasoned with salt, pepper and butter, add to it sufficient rich white sauce to make about 2 cupfuls in all. Take small ramekins, butter them well, place a little chopped parsley, a drop or two of onion juice, and a teaspoonful of finely chopped mushrooms previously cooked in butter, in each ramekin, and break an egg on this in each; season with salt and pepper and put the cases in a pan containing hot water; put the pan in a fairly hot oven and leave it there until the eggs are set but not hard. Dish up the hot spinach in an Entrée dish, place the croûtons on the spinach and carefully turn out one egg upon each croûton. Serve with thin slices of ham.

Foie de veau En Brochettes

Cut the liver in 2-inch squares about 1 inch thick. Season on all sides with salt and pepper. Thread on a skewer alternately with pieces of rather fat bacon of the same size, but thinner. Roll the prepared Brochettes in a little oil and grill on all sides until crisp and brown. The Brochettes may also be dipped in beaten egg and breadcrumbs, if preferred that way, and fried in butter.

Savory Potatoes

Add a tablespoon of chopped watercress and chopped fresh mint leaves to some mashed potatoes, then a few pats of butter, and brown under the grill.

Grilled Tomatoes

Brush over some smallish, firm Tomatoes with softened butter or olive oil. Dust with pepper and salt and cook slowly under grill.

Apple Fool

Cook a quart of apples in a light sugar syrup till tender. Rub through a sieve, and when quite cold add a pint of whipped cream. Taste and add sugar if you think that it is necessary. Serve quite cold.

MENU VI

Mushroom Omelette

*   *   *

Cold Asparagus, Vinaigrette Sauce

*   *   *

Braised Ox Tongue, Sauce piquante

*   *   *

Epinards à la Creme

*   *   *

Cheese Board

*   *   *

Coffee

The first wine might well be one of the fragrant white wines of the Moselle, either a Bernkasteler, a Piesporter or a Wehlener and the second a nice Claret, an older wine than the white if possible, either a Château Pontet-Canet from the Médoc, or a Château Pape-Clément, from the Graves de Bordeaux, or a Château la Gaffelière-Naudes, from St. Emilion, any of them would partner very well indeed both the meat and the cheese.

RECIPES

Mushroom Omelette

Pick, wash, trim, peel the mushrooms; cut them up, caps and stalks alike, and toss them in butter over a good fire until done; season well with salt and pepper and keep hot. Make an omelette in the usual way, and at the time of dishing the omelette, fold the mushrooms in it, keeping a few to put on top of it by way of decoration.

Ox Tongue

1 Ox Tongue
Onions
2 peeled tomatoes
Bouillon or stock
Salt and pepper
2 cloves of garlic
Some fresh pork skin
Carrots
1 glass white wine
Bouquet garni

Choose a nice plump tongue with smooth skin. Soak it in cold water for about 12 hours, changing the water once or twice if the tongue is salted or dried. Wash well, trim off root, removing hard nerve. Take a heavy iron stewing pot. Place at the bottom of it the fresh pork skin strips (*couennes*), and cover them with thick slices of onions and carrots. Lay the tongue on this 'bed,' cover the pot and put it on the fire. Cook until the vegetables begin to brown, turning the tongue now and then; add the tomatoes, cut in pieces, and the white wine. Cook gently until the wine has been reduced to half its original quantity, then moisten with water or stock or both mixed together, so that the liquid comes half-way to the tongue. Then add the bouquet garni, the garlic and pepper; cover closely the pot and simmer its contents for 3 or 4 hours, when the tongue will be quite tender. Skim off fat; remove the garlic and bouquet garni; slice the tongue and serve the slices on a hot dish with a *Sauce Piquante*.

Sauce Piquante

2 oz. butter
4 oz. chopped onions
4 tablespoons salt and pepper
1 or 2 vinegar pickles
White wine

Gently melt the butter in a copper or earthenware saucepan until it begins to smoke slightly, then throw in the onions and stir, cooking them until they are of a rather dark golden color. Now add the flour, stirring until the whole mixture is evenly brown. Moisten with white wine, pouring it little by little and stirring well all the time. Season and let it all simmer over a low heat for 15 or 20 minutes. Cut up one or two vinegar gherkins, and add them to the sauce with some chopped parsley, chervil and tarragon; simmer for 5 or 10 minutes longer. Add some of the gravy from the meat being cooked at the time or a little good essence of meat, just enough to get the right consistency of the sauce.

Epinards à la Crème

Trim, wash, and cook the required quantity of spinach; then chop or sieve it and put it into a fireproof dish with 2 ounces butter per pound of spinach, and stir well over a quick fire until all the moisture has disappeared. Then add as much fresh cream as you can spare; season with pepper and salt and a little nutmeg; if in the mood for an experiment add also a pinch of sugar. Stir well and simmer for 8 or 10 minutes more, and serve hot.

MENU VII

Oeufs Marie

*   *   *

Moules Marinière

*   *   *

Roast Duckling and Garden Peas

*   *   *

Raspberry Whip

For this Luncheon, one could begin with one of the few really dry white wines of Germany, a Steinwein from Franconia, a Randersacker Spielberg, for instance: it would partner excellently not only the eggs and the Moules, but also the duckling, and it could be followed by a richer, more luscious white wine from the Palatinate, a Forster Jesuitengarten Spätlese, which would be a better match for the Raspberries and leave a sweeter taste in the mouth.

RECIPES

Oeufs Marie

Hard boiled eggs sliced and served with sliced cooked beets as a Hors d'oeuvre, dressed with oil and vinegar, salt and pepper, chopped chervil, chives and capers, and diced fillets of anchovies in oil.

Moules Marinière

First of all make up a Court-Bouillon with white wine, vinegar and various culinary herbs—chervil, parsley, tarragon chiefly, leaving to simmer for half an hour: strain and put back on the fire; put then in the pan the mussels which have been carefully cleaned so that there is no sand left in them. Cover the pan closely until the mussels are cooked. Take them out of the pan one by one on the half shell and put them into a soup tureen or a deep serving dish, then pour over them the liquor in which they were cooked.

Roast Duckling

Sprinkle with pepper and salt a cleaned, dressed and trussed duckling. Spread a little softened butter over its back. Roast in hot oven, allowing 15 minutes per pound of the trussed bird's weight, and baste now and again. All kinds of stuffing may be put into the duckling before it goes into the oven, but a young and tender bird is far better without any such highly flavored stuff as most stuffings are made of. The same may be said of the usual orange salad served with duck and duckling; it may help a lame duck which is rather greasy, but a nice little duckling is better without it. All it asks for is a generous helping of fresh garden peas.

Garden Peas

There is no denying that deep-freeze Peas are very good indeed: there is no other vegetable that can put up with deep freeze better than green peas: they are tender and, with just a little assistance in the kitchen, they are tasty and really good: but they have not got and they cannot ever have the flavor and sweetness of freshly gathered garden peas: these, unfortunately, are not available for more than a very few weeks during the summer.

Garden peas may be cooked and served in two different ways, the English and the French. This is the English way: Shell the peas, wash them, and put them in plenty of salted boiling water; add a sprig or two of mint and a pinch of sugar; then cover the pan. When the water comes to the boil again, take the pan away from the fire and go on simmering until the peas be tender. Drain at once, dish the peas in a warmed dish, season with salt and pepper, ram a piece of fresh butter in the middle of the peas and serve hot.

And this is the French way: Peel 2 or 3 small onions and toss them in hot butter in a deep pan for a few moments; then put into the pan a head of Romaine Lettuce (washed first, of course), a lump of sugar, a spoonful of warm water, and a quart of garden peas, shelled and washed. Cover the pan and cook on a gentle heat, shaking the pan occasionally, for about 20 minutes, when the peas should be ready to serve.

Raspberry Whip

Mash a quart of fresh ripe red Raspberries in a bowl with plenty of sifted sugar. Add the unbeaten whites of 2 eggs, mix well and then beat the lot stiffly to a froth. Chill and serve with whipped cream.

MENU VIII

Melon Cantaloup

*　　*　　*

Lobster Beaugency

*　　*　　*

Rognons à la Berrichonne, Pommes soufflées

*　　*　　*

Strawberries and Raspberries in red wine

The first wine to be served might well be one of the really dry and lighter Sherries, a Manzanilla, or better still, a Macharnudo la Riva, well chilled, of course, which would not only be acceptable with the sweet Melon but should also be quite a good match for the lobster. With the kidneys and the mixed fruit, a fairly stout wine would be best to follow the Sherry, such as a Chateauneuf-du-Pape, for instance.

RECIPES

Lobster Beaugency

Prepare a court-bouillon (page 26) and put in it a live lobster with its claws safely tied to the body; cover the pan and put on the fire. Cook from 20 to 30 minutes, according to the size of the lobster, after it has come to the boil, reducing the heat after the first 10 minutes. Let the lobster cool in the court-bouillon, and do not use an iron pan; if you do, the meat of the lobster will be just as good but dark and not appetizing. When cold, split the lobster in two and dice the meat. Heat about 2 tablespoons of butter and fry the pieces of lobster in it for a few moments; add a glassful of dry Sherry and gradually, ½ pint of fresh cream and 2 tablespoons of a well seasoned cream sauce. Simmer gently for 10 minutes, then remove pan from the fire. Beat 2 egg yolks with a little more cream and a tablespoon of melted butter, and mix this with the lobster. Use this mixture to fill up the empty shells of the lobster; bake in a hot oven until bubbling and brown slightly; then serve piping hot.

Rognons à la Berrichonne

Lamb's kidneys
Butter
Fried croûtons
Red wine
Salt and pepper
Meat extract or meat glaze if available
Salt pork
Fresh mushroom caps
Tiny "button" onions

Skin and cut the kidneys in halves. Toss them in sizzling butter and, when done, place them upon fried croûtons. Pour half a glass of red wine into the pan in which the kidneys have just been cooked; season and stir over a good heat until there is but about half of the original wine left in the pan: then add a little butter and, if available, some meat extract or meat glaze. Cover the kidneys with this gravy and serve them around a small *ragoût* of fried cubes of pork, *sautés* mushroom caps and glazed "button" onions.

Pommes Soufflées

Choose some firm, waxy potatoes of medium size. Peel them and slice them roundways as thin as you can, all of the same thickness. Do not wash them: just wipe them well in a clean cloth. To make sure of success you should have two deep pans ready, each with some deep boiling fat at different temperatures. Plunge the potatoes into the first pan, in fat at a temperature of not more than 350°F., let them cook 4 or 5 minutes, shaking the pan or stirring the potatoes all the time; when they rise to the surface and begin to puff, skim them and transfer them at once to the second pan where the fat should be very hot and smoking, about 400°F. They will puff at once but should be left and stirred until they begin to brown. Then is the time to drain them and serve them at once with a dusting of salt over them.

MENU IX

Mackerel

*   *   *

Baked Eggs Columbus

*   *   *

Fricandeau de Veau, Creamed Spinach

*   *   *

Cheese Board

*   *   *

Coffee

Two Swiss white wines should prove quite suitable for this meal, the first might be either a Fendant du Valais or a Neuchâtel, quite young wines of the last vintage, whilst the second ought to be a little older, a two-year-old which is quite old enough for most Swiss white wines, and from the Lavaux ridge, either Epesses or Dézaley.

RECIPES

Mackerel

Remove heads from 3 or 4 medium-sized mackerels. Clean and split open. Lay them in an earthenware baking dish. Add a good sprinkling of salt and pepper (a few whole peppercorns are best), as well as a little dry thyme and a broken-up bay leaf. Cut an onion into thin rings and finely chop some parsley. Sprinkle this over the fish, adding also a few thin slices of carrot. Barely cover with a mixture of water and wine-vinegar, or, better still, some dry, rather sharp white wine and a good squeeze of lemon. Bake in a rather slow oven until the vegetables are done, basting frequently. Allow to cool in the liquor, removing peppercorns, herbs and slices of carrot when serving. Serve when quite cold.

Eggs Columbus

Small, firm tomatoes or green peppers
Salt and pepper
Butter
Fresh eggs
Squares of toast
Tomato sauce

Plunge the tomatoes or peppers into boiling water and slip off the skins. Drain and dry well. Cut each one around stem and remove seeds and hard parts. Sprinkle interiors with salt and pepper. Put each tomato or pepper in a small buttered pan. Break a fresh egg into each, season and bake in a moderate oven for about 12 minutes or until eggs are set. Put one tomato or pepper carefully on squares of hot buttered toast and serve with tomato sauce, which may be handed separately or poured over the eggs.

Fricandeau de Veau

2 or 3 lb. veal
Salt and pepper
Carrots
Bouquet-garni
Lardons of larding bacon
A thin slice of fresh pork fat
Onions
2 cups good meat stock

The best meat for this dish is the best veal, that is the fillet. Season the *lardons* with salt and pepper and "lard" the meat; then wrap it completely in the thin slice of fresh pork fat *(barde de lard)* and put it in a heavy iron or earthenware braising pan with the vegetables and the *bouquet garni,* adding salt, pepper, and the stock. Cook gently, the pot being covered, for from 3 to 4 hours. Remove the cover and increase the heat; cook the meat uncovered turning it frequently to "dry out." Skim off the fat and serve the veal with its own gravy, sliced crossways, and with creamed spinach.

Creamed Spinach

Trim 4 pounds freshly picked spinach, discarding the whole of the stalks; wash it well in several waters. Put it dripping wet in a saucepan, without any other water, and leave it on a slow fire for half an hour, when it will have gone down a good deal in volume. Make a *roux blond* with some butter and half its weight of flour, and mix this with the spinach. Then add a quart of good meat stock, season with pepper and salt and a good pinch of sugar; cover the pan and leave it in a moderate oven for 45 minutes. Put the spinach through a sieve, then re-heat it and bind it with 4 or 5 yolks of eggs beaten in a little fresh cream and some butter.

MENU X

Avocado Pear

*   *   *

Crab Omelette

*   *   *

Rôti de Porc en Casserole, Pommes Purée

*   *   *

Salade verte

*   *   *

Cheese Board

*   *   *

Coffee

The Avocado Pear is really best, provided the fruit be quite ripe, with no other dressing than a squeeze of lemon. Treated thus it is also better for the wine than when treated with a vinegar dressing, but even then one of the less expensive white Burgundies would be best, a plain Mâcon Blanc, for instance, and it would be quite good enough to serve with the Omelette. With the main dish, however, a better wine should be chosen, not one of the great aristocrats, perhaps, but a white Burgundy with a fair amount of body as well as some distinction, such as a white Morey St. Denis or a Beaune, Clos des Mouches: either would partner the roast and the cheese.

RECIPES

Crab Omelette

Remove carefully all the meat from the shell of a freshly boiled crab, separating the soft and darker part from the white meat, and add it to the beaten eggs when ready to make the omelette. Pour the mixture of beaten eggs and soft crab meat into the sizzling butter of the omelette pan; reduce the heat; cook gently as you would any ordinary omelette, not forgetting salt and pepper; you might add just a dash of Cayenne pepper in the seasoning. When the omelette is ready to serve, slip it upon a hot dish and fold into it the white meat of the crab, which you will heat in butter first.

Rôti de Porc en Casserole

One must always bear in mind that Pork should not be cooked quickly, or it will become tough, stringy and indigestible. Use a heavy iron or earthenware casserole with a tightly fitting lid. Put in the casserole a couple of tablespoons of butter and, when hot, brown in it the joint on all sides. Season with salt and pepper and just a very small crushed clove of garlic; lightly dredge with flour, brown in a hot oven until nicely colored all over, then reduce heat and cook the meat very slowly in the covered casserole, turning it fairly frequently, until the butter is clear and there is a rich, brown sediment at the bottom of the casserole; add a little hot water and rub the meat against the sides of the casserole to scrape off the sediment. Pour a rich gravy over the meat at the time of serving, whether served whole as a joint, or sliced.

Pommes Purée

Choose whenever possible some of the white, floury potatoes rather than the yellow, waxy sorts. Peel and boil them and when done press them through a sieve. Put back the sieved potatoes into a pan on the fire; season with salt and pepper; add a piece of butter and stir it in; add also as much hot milk as will make it possible to whip the *purée* to the consistency of thick cream.

MENU XI

Lobster Patties

*　　*　　*

Roast Grouse, Chip Potatoes and Watercress

*　　*　　*

Beignets de Céleri

*　　*　　*

Greengages and Green Figs

*　　*　　*

Coffee

With the Lobster Patties a youngish but well-bred white Burgundy like a Meursault Genevrieres would be very nice, and it would prove a most suitable introduction to a really great red Burgundy that would be a match for the finest game bird in the world, a young grouse: a Musigny, Chambertin or Richebourg of a good vintage would be admirable. As an anti-climax, with the luscious fully ripe Greengages and green figs, just a glass of chilled Sauternes, not necessarily the very finest of them, but a good wine like Château la Tour Blanche or Château Doizy-Védrines, would most likely prove quite popular.

RECIPES

Lobster Patties

Patties shells and vol-au-vent cases are much better bought ready-made from the pastry chefs who specialize in them, and here is how to make the filling for them:

Diced boiled lobster meat
Thick Béchamel sauce
Yolks of eggs
Mushroom caps
Butter
Sherry
Lemon juice

Add the diced lobster to the sauce and heat well in a double-boiler. Beat the egg yolks with the cream. Fry the mushroom caps in butter, slice them and add them and the butter in which they were cooked to the lobster and sauce mixture. Season with pepper and salt, and flavor with some dry Sherry and a squeeze of lemon when ready to fill the cases and serve.

Roast Grouse

There is no better game bird, gastronomically speaking, than a young Grouse three or four days after it is shot: it must not be too fresh nor should it be allowed to get 'high.' Pluck, singe, draw, and truss as you would a chicken. Season inside and out with pepper and salt; insert a little butter and a twig of lovage or summer savory inside, if available, but on no account any thyme, bay leaf or any other strongly scented herb. Slip on the bird a waistcoat of thin rashers of fat bacon, and roast in a hot oven for 15 minutes, or maybe 18 if the bird be rather large. It must not be raw, of course, but pink or slightly underdone. Baste frequently with the bacon fat during cooking, then remove the bacon rashers, dredge lightly with flour and put back into the oven for a very little while, just long enough to brown the bird's breast, and then serve hot on a piece of toast which should be slipped under the bird to catch the gravy that drops from it during cooking.

Beignets de Céleri

Scrape the required quantity of celery stalks and boil them in acidulated water until tender; drain and dry them; cut them up in 3-in. lengths; dip each length in batter and fry in boiling fat until crisp and brown. Drain on paper and serve at once, piled criss-cross, with fried parsley as garnish.

MENU XII

Jambon de Parme et Melon

* * *

Truite au Bleu

* * *

Perdrix aux Choux

* * *

Salade Lorette

* * *

Cheese Omelette

A light, youngish, fragrant German white wine of fine quality, such as a Kaseler Kehrnagel of Reichsgraf von Kesselstatt's bottling and shipping would be excellent as a first wine with both hors d'oeuvre and fish, and it might be followed by an older, bigger and really great Hock, such as a Schloss Vollrads, Estate bottled by Graf Matuschka Greiffenclau, served with the bird and the cheese omelette.

RECIPES

Truite au Bleu

Clean the trout but do not attempt to scale it. Put it in a dish with a little vinegar which will 'blue' it; with more vinegar, some white wine and whatever garden herbs you happen to have, make a sharp and well flavored court-bouillon (page 26); put it on the fire and when it is boiling slip the trout in it. As soon as it comes to the boil again, draw the pan away from the fire and cover it closely. Let it stand covered for about five minutes, then remove the fish carefully, draining it well, and serve it forth with whatever sauce you fancy. The fish itself has no taste, or practically none, but it has the right consistency to show off a good Hollandaise or any other well balanced sauce.

Perdrix aux Choux

1 partridge
1 thick rasher of bacon
Chipolata sausages
2 or 3 carrots
Thin slices of fat salt pork
1 medium size white cabbage
Bouquet garni
Salt, pepper and a little powdered mace
2 cups bouillon or stock

This is usually the way an old bird is made not only tender but very good, indeed. It is obvious, however, that a young bird will be even more tender and very much better than an old one. Prepare the bird as for roasting. Shred the cabbage finely. Cover the birds breast with the thin slices of fat salt pork. Cut the bacon into dice and cook gently to extract all the fat, removing the lean portions when this has been done. Brown the bird on all sides in the bacon fat. Add salt and pepper and a very small pinch of powdered mace, as well as the *bouquet garni*. Add the stock or bouillon, cover the pan, and cook the bird gently until tender. The carrots should be sliced and put in the pan under and around the bird. When the bird has been simmering for about an hour, put in the shredded cabbage which you will have blanched previously in plenty of salted boiling water. Let the cabbage cook gently and thoroughly so that it absorbs the juices from the partridge. When done, serve the bird on a bed of cabbage and with the chipolata sausages, previously fried or baked separately; also with the bacon cooked at the same time but cut up in pieces and set round the dish with the chipolata. Serve boiled potatoes separately or in the same dish as a garnish.

Salade Lorette

Very small leaves of Corn Salad (Fr. Mâche) mixed with some pieces of cooked red beets and fine sticks of uncooked celery.

Cheese Omelette

Use one tablespoon of grated Swiss or Parmesan cheese—or both mixed—to 4 eggs. Beat the eggs, add the grated cheese, beat the mixture vigorously and make the omelette with it in the usual way. A little more grated cheese may be sprinkled over the surface of the omelette at the time of serving.

MENU XIII

Oeufs Joinville

*　　　*　　　*

Skewered Smelts

*　　　*　　　*

Poulet Chasseur

*　　　*　　　*

Salade verte

*　　　*　　　*

Cheese Board

With the hors d'oeuvre and the fish a nicely chilled white Graves such as a Château la Louvière or Château Olivier would be quite acceptable, and it could be followed by one of the fine red wines also of Graves, either a Château Smith-Haut-Lafitte or a Château Malaritc-Lagralière, unless the occasion should justify calling for a Château Haut-Brion, a finer and, of course, a dearer wine.

RECIPES

Oeufs Joinville

A rather different way of serving hard-boiled eggs as a hors d'oeuvre: the eggs are sliced and served with a pretty 'pink' Mayonnaise over them. The pink of the sauce is easy to obtain by coloring an ordinary Mayonnaise sauce with pounded and sieved *unshelled* prawns.

Skewered Smelts

Clean the Smelts; remove their heads and tails; cut the fish into ½-inch slices, crossways. Cut some thin rashers of bacon into pieces of the same size. Skewer fish and bacon alternately, brush over with either olive oil or oiled butter; season with salt and pepper; roll in crumbs and grill, turning frequently; or else fry in deep fat.

Poulet Chasseur

1 *chicken*
1 *tablespoon butter*
1 *clove garlic*
1 *or 2 shallots*
2 *cups good stock*
1 *glass dry Sherry or dry white wine*
2 *tablespoons tomato Purée*
Chopped Fines Herbs
1 *tablespoon olive oil*
Salt and pepper
Croûtons

Cut the chicken into serving pieces and brown them in mixed oil and butter previously heated, together with minced garlic and shallots. When the pieces of chicken will all be nicely brown, add the stock, the wine and the tomato purée; season with salt and pepper, sprinkle the chopped *Fines Herbs*—chervil and parsley mostly—then cover the pan and cook rather quickly for about half an hour, that is until the chicken is done and tender. Strain gravy over chicken and serve with hot *croûtons* and sautés or grilled mushrooms.

MENU XIV

Oysters

*　　*　　*

Tournedos Dauphinoise, Pommes Anna

*　　*　　*

Pâté de Caneton, Salade

*　　*　　*

Cheese Board

With the oysters, freshly opened and served on the deep shell, the traditional wine to serve is a Chablis. It is unfortunate that the name of Chablis should have caught the popular fancy to such an extent because the Chablis vineyards are not nearly large enough to meet the world-wide demand for Chablis. To make sure that one gets a genuine Chablis it is well to get a wine which bears the name of one of the good Chablis vineyards such as Chablis Valmur, Chablis Mont de Milieu, Chablis Vaulorent, and so forth. With the Tournedos one would naturally turn to Bordeaux and choose one of those beautifully balanced and elegant Clarets from the Médoc vineyards, such as a Château Rausan-Ségla, or a Château Beychevelle, or a Château Calon-Ségur, any of them would partner happily the beef, the Pâté and the cheese. Of course, should one be in the mood for a match between Bordeaux and Burgundy, one could very well serve a red wine from the Côte de Nuits, a Grands Echézeaux, for instance, after the Claret.

RECIPES

Tournedos Dauphinoise

Tender, rather thick, individual Tournedos
½ lb. fresh mushrooms
1 tablespoon flour
2 tablespoonfuls butter
½ cup thick cream
Salt and pepper
Croûtons

Pan-fry or grill the Tournedos, black outside and pink inside: keep them hot. Peel the mushrooms, toss them in butter until cooked; reduce heat and add the cream which should have been previously blended with the flour; season well with pepper and salt. To serve turn the mushrooms *purée* into a hot dish, add as many fried *Croûtons* as there are Tournedos, place a Tournedos on each *croûton,* and pour over them the gravy or sauce made from the drippings saved from the cooking tournedos. Serve hot.

Pommes Anna

Peel the potatoes; cut them in very thin rings; soak in water for 10 or 15 minutes; drain them and dry them in a cloth. Take a straight-sided fireproof dish (with a lid) just large enough to take all the potatoes, and butter it well. Arrange the potatoes in it in layers; season with salt and pepper; dot them here and there with butter with a lavish hand. When the dish is full, spread the top layer with butter, put on the lid, and make it airtight with some paste made with flour and water. Bake in a slack oven for three quarters of an hour; turn out what looks like a half cooked potato cake and put it back in the dish upside down. Cover closely again and go on cooking for another three quarters of an hour, and you should have by then a beautiful golden potato cake to serve with the Tournedos.

Pâté de Caneton

Choose a young but meaty duckling and roast it for about 20 minutes only; it should be not done but sufficiently under-done by then for your purpose. Lift the whole of the breast in long and very thin slivers. But first of all you should prepare the right forcemeat like this: lightly and quickly fry some fat bacon and some calf's liver; remove from the pan and swill the pan with some Madeira; pound the liver and bacon, mois-tening with the Madeira from the pan; incorporate the pounded meat of the legs, etc. of the duckling; work in some yolk of egg; season with pepper and salt and a very little thyme and powdered bay leaf. Now line a buttered pie dish with short pastry but remember to make a small slit at the bottom. Lay in alternately the forcemeat and the neatly arranged slivers of duckling. Finish with a layer of forcemeat. Put on a covering layer of pastry, providing a small escape for the steam by mak-ing a slit in the top. Bake for about one hour. Turn out the pie upside down upon the hot dish on which it is to be served. Slice off the top—originally the bottom, horizontally, and cut it up into as many pieces as there are guests at the table. Pour over the exposed forcemeat some hot Madeira sauce, rather thicker than usual, and serve a slice of pie on each piece of crust. This is quite good when eaten hot, but it is just as good the next day when eaten cold.

MENU XV

L'Omelette du Baron de Barante

*   *   *

Grilled Chops and fried Potatoes

*   *   *

Salade Verte

*   *   *

Cheese Board

The first wine might well be a fresh Rosé wine, either a Tavel or a Cabernet Rosé d'Anjou, followed by a red wine from the Rhône Valley, should Tavel be chosen as first wine, a Château Fortia, for instance, which is a Premier Grand Cru of Châteauneuf-du-Pape; or one of the red wines of Touraine, such as a Chinon or a Bourgueuil, should the Cabernet d'Anjou be the leader. The only difficulty is that Touraine wines are not easy to come by outside the Loire Valley, whereas the red wines of the Rhône Valley, and more particularly the wines of Châteauneuf-du-Pape are quoted by many although not all wine-merchants.

RECIPES

L'Omelette du Baron de Barante

This is probably the most glamorous omelette of all: it was the favorite omelette of Edward VI and also of Horace Annesley Vachell. This is the recipe given by Vachell himself: Peel carefully 1½ pounds of fresh mushrooms. Cut them into slices so that they can be cooked easily. Sprinkle with salt and cook in best butter. When they are a pale yellow, pour over them a glass of good Port. Cover the saucepan and reduce by half. Then add fresh, thick cream, and 12 slices of the tail of a lobster which has been cooked in a court-bouillon (page 26). Cover the stewpan and let the whole simmer. Place this mixture in an 18-egg omelette; fold the omelette, sprinkle it liberally with grated Parmesan, and brown to a rich golden in a quick oven.

Grilled Chops

There are single and double grilled lamb chops—the double ones are best—and there are at least a hundred and one different ways of serving them, plain or garnished. The simplest, and many people believe the best way to deal with chops is to cook them under a grill unadorned or after they have been dipped in egg and breadcrumbs. The most extravagant way is rightly called 'à la millionnaire' and this is how (they say) it is done: Two out of three chops must be cut rather thin and the third much thicker. Season all three and tie or skewer them firmly together, the thick one between the two thin ones. Cook under a fierce heat, turning them about all the time so that the juices from the two outside thin chops may penetrate the thick one in the center. Then serve the center chop and give away the two outside ones!

Fried Potatoes

Whenever possible one should get some of the yellow, waxy potatoes for frying; they are so much better than the white, mealy sorts which are best for boiling or baking. Olive oil is very good for frying potatoes, but there are now other kinds of fats available which give also very good results. Cut the sticks of potatoes as near as possible of the same size and thickness and put them, not too many at the same time, into the hot oil or fat when it is beginning to smoke, or when at a temperature of 375°F. if you have a frying thermometer. Fry until crisp and golden; take them out and keep hot on white kitchen paper whilst you cook another lot, shaking and stirring to prevent sticking. When ready to serve, sprinkle some salt over them.

DINNERS

MENU XVI

Velouté à l'Oseille or Crème Forestière

* * *

Carrelet (Flounder) Meunière

* * *

Poulet à l'Estragon

* * *

Poire Cardinal

This is the sort of Menu which people might choose who prefer white wines to red: it could be served with a fairly full bodied white Burgundy such as a Chassagne-Montrachet bottled at the Domaine by a reputable firm; and a glass of a rather sweet Sauternes like a Chateau Climens with the Pear. But it is also the type of Menu which could be served to everybody's satisfaction with Champagne from beginning to end.

RECIPES

Velouté à L'Oseille

Take 4 handfuls of freshly picked Sorrel; remove all stalks and ribs; wash in several waters and put in a pan dripping wet, without any more water, but with a tablespoonful of butter. Leave pan on a moderate heat, stirring the Sorrel which will soon melt; add 1½ pints of milk, little by little; season with pepper and salt and bring to the boil. In the meantime, fry some snippets of bread, and beat 2 yolks of eggs in some fresh cream. Warm the soup tureen; put the fried snippets of bread in it; then the cream with the beaten yolks of eggs; and last the boiling sorrel soup; stir well and serve.

Crème Forestière

Clean and chop (but do not peel) ½ pound mushroom; boil them very gently in a cup of water for 25 minutes; melt 4 tablespoons of butter in a heavy pan; brown lightly in it a sliced carrot, a sliced onion, a sprig of parsley, and a sliced stalk of celery. Shake over the pan 2 tablespoons of flour; stir till it disappears in the butter; then add 1 quart of scalded milk, stirring until it thickens. Season and keep hot. Drain the mushrooms, saving the liquor, and mash them to a purée. Strain the milk soup and add the mushroom purée to it; check the seasoning; reheat, and serve with a teaspoon of whipped cream and a light dusting of paprika.

Carrelet Meunière

For this dish one must get a flounder, and one must also have a pan large enough to deal with the fish whole. Season the fish with salt and pepper and dust it all over with a little flour. Heat some butter in a large pan and when the butter will be just boiling, put the fish into it: turn it over after a minutes or so, then once again a little later. When the fish is cooked—that is when a skewer goes right through fairly easily—put the flounder on a hot dish, squeeze some lemon juice over, sprinkle a little pepper and salt, and—that is where the *Meunière* comes in—pour hot melted butter over it all just at the time of serving.

Poulet a L'estragon

Fresh Tarragon leaves
3 tablespoons Butter
1 fine plump chicken
Hot stock or water
Salt and pepper

2 carrots
Small pinch of thyme
1 or 2 onions
1 clove
Short stem Tarragon

Chop the tarragon leaves and mix with the butter; place this inside the fowl and sew it up neatly. Place the bird in a heavy iron pot with enough stock or bouillon (failing which water) to come up to half the side of the fowl. Add the other vegetables—carrots and onions, as well as the thyme, clove and branch tarragon. Cook the bird gently until tender, and when done remove its skin and keep it hot, but do not let it get dry. Make a nicely balanced sauce with the liquor from the pot, add chopped tarragon leaves and pour it over the white chicken, decorating the edges with more tarragon leaves.

Poires Cardinal

Peel and poach some smallish pears in sugar and water; let them get cold in the syrup in which they were poached. When cold, serve them with a generous coating of strawberry purée flavored with a little kirsch or maraschino.

MENU XVII

Bisque de Homard

*　　*　　*

Sole Colbert

*　　*　　*

Tournedos Rossini, Cèpes à la Bordelaise

*　　*　　*

Lemon-water Ice Wafers

*　　*　　*

Fruit

With the lobster soup a glass of cold and really dry Fino
Sherry would surely be welcome, but with the Sole Colbert one
could hardly do better than partnering it with a delicate white
Burgundy such as a Meursault Goutte d'Or: it is a wine which
has breed and charm, but it is not assertive and would in no
way interfere with the appreciation of the Claret which should
be served with the Tournedos, not any 'ordinaire' Claret but
one of the great ones, such as a Château Lafitte or a Château
Belair, should one prefer St. Emilion to the Medoc. With the
ice and fruit, just one glass of one of the luscious Palatinate
white wines, such as a Deidesheimer Hofstuck, would be rather
nice.

RECIPES

Bisque de Homard

The basis of all Bisques is a highly seasoned *Court-Bouillon*
of white wine, (Sherry is best) in which the fish is left over-
night to marinate before being cooked with some fresh toma-

toes. When it is cooked, the lobster-meat is pounded in a mortar to a smooth cream, and what goes through the sieve is put back in the pot and left to simmer quite gently for a very long time. When the Bisque is ready to serve, first put in the warmed soup tureen 2 or 3 lightly beaten egg yolks, a little fresh cream and a glassful of Sherry; pour the soup on it all and stir well; then serve hot.

Sole Colbert

Cut off the head and remove the black skin of the sole. Detach fillets from the bone with the point of a sharp knife and break up the bone in two or three places so that it may be removed more easily when the sole has been cooked. Dip the sole in milk, then dust it over with very little flour. Shake it well. Dip it in egg and breadcrumbs and fry in a very hot fat for 10 or 12 minutes according to the size of the fish. When cooked, lay the sole on a cloth or white paper on the shelf of an open oven to drain off any excess of fat. The sole should then be put on a hot dish, its broken backbone is removed, a Maitre d'Hôtel Butter is put in its place, and the sole is served at once.

Tournedos Rossini

This is a delicious and costly way to deal with a *Tournedos,* and it cannot be attempted unless or until one has secured some *foie gras* and some truffles. Choose the required number of thick tender *Tournedos* of best beef and well hung, and grill them in the usual way. Then place on each *Tournedos* a thin slice of *Foie Gras,* previously dipped first in milk, then in flour, and gently tossed in butter for a couple of minutes. Add to meat drippings and gravy as much port wine as you fancy, and as many slices of truffles as you can afford. Simmer gently for a little while only, then serve the *Tournedos* on hot fried *Croûtons,* with the slice of *Foie Gras* on each *Tournedos,* and a slice of black Truffle in the centre of the *Foie Gras.*

Cèpes à la Bordelaise

Cèpes are the most popular of the many members of the **Boletus** family of edible mushrooms; they are found in plenty, from May until the first frosts of the winter in October or November; they are quite common in woods and spinneys but very few if any people dare pick them and eat them: they look rather deadly and yet they are quite safe as well as delicious. There is no difficulty, however, in getting *Cèpes* from France, at all times of the year, in tins or cans.

Drain off the liquid in which *Cèpes* are kept in tins; cut off stems and chop them finely with some shallots and a clove of garlic, more or less, according to personal taste. Pour a couple of tablespoonfuls of good olive oil in a frying pan, and as soon as it is smoking hot, fry in it the *Cèpes* caps, cutting up the larger ones into two or even three pieces. Let them simmer gently for about ten minutes and then add the chopped stems, season with salt and pepper. Continue to cook until the oil be quite clear, and the *Cèpes* will then be ready to serve: add at the last moment a little chopped parsley and a squeeze of lemon juice.

Lemon-Water Ice

To a quart of cold water put ½ pound sifted sugar and the juice of 3 large lemons; also grate in the rind of one large or two small lemons: beat well together for five minutes; go by the look of the syrup and add a little sifted sugar if it looks to watery. Then strain through a sieve into the freezer, put on the cover and take out when soft-frozen.

Wafers

Wafers are the thinnest and lightest of all biscuits; they are usually sweetened. All biscuit makers have their own registered brands of Wafers made according to their own recipes, and all of them are better and cheaper than any kind of wafer any housewife could make herself with flour, eggs, water and sugar.

MENU XVIII

Mushroom soup

* * *

Halibut Fillets

* * *

Veal Olives and Broad Beans Purée

* * *

Asparagus and melted Butter

* * *

Gâteau Mille-Feuille and Fruit

This Menu might very well be chosen for a dinner when some good German wines were to be served. Rising from the lightest to the biggest, a Longuicher Maximiner Herrenberg would make a modest but gracious beginning and partner both soup and fish. With the Veal, a Hochheimer Kirchenstuck Riesling Auslese would be quite acceptable, a wine with greater breed, fuller and richer without being sweet. With the dessert, should your guests be connoisseurs, you could not do better than give them a Niersteiner Pettenthal 2nd. Terrasse Allerfeinste Goldbeerenauslese, Estate bottled Anton Balbach Erben, a truly magnificent wine.

RECIPES

Mushroom Soup
> *1 quart fresh Mushrooms*
> *2 ounces butter*
> *½ cup cream*
> *Salt and pepper*
> *Dash of nutmeg*
> *Bouquet garni*

Wash but do not peel the mushrooms; put them in water with a dash of vinegar in it, bring to the boil, and then simmer slowly until the mushrooms are soft enough to be rubbed through a sieve. This will give you a mushroom *purée* which you will set aside and keep warm. In the meantime, put the butter in a pan over a slow fire, and as it melts, sift the flour into the pan and work it with a wooden spoon into a smooth paste; then add gradually the required quantity of hot milk and water in equal proportions, stirring all the while over a good heat; season with pepper and salt, and just a dusting of nutmeg; put in a bouquet garni (in a muslin bag). When the soup comes to the boil, fish out the muslin bag of herbs, and put in the mushroom *purée,* stirring well; when the soup comes to the boil again, add the cream, stir well in and serve hot. Small square pieces of stale bread fried in fat are sometimes put in this soup at time of serving.

Halibut Fillets

Halibut, 1½ or 2 lb.
Court-Bouillon
2 tablespoons butter
2 tablespoons flour
1 blade or pinch mace
Salt and pepper
Butter or dripping to fry the fillets
1 teaspoon lemon juice

Put the fish in a well flavored Court-Bouillon (page 26) and let it simmer very slowly for about 10 minutes. Remove fish; take off its skin and the bones; cut up into fillets. Melt the butter in a pan, add the flour, mix well and moisten with some of the Court-Bouillon after it has been strained. Season with pepper and salt and mace. Heat some more butter or some dripping in a frying pan; fry the fillets of halibut in it; season with salt and pepper. When the fish is light brown on all sides, remove from the frying pan but let it go on simmering in another pan, in the sauce made for it, until thoroughly well cooked. Put the fillets upon a hot serving dish, season them with lemon juice, and pour over them the sauce in which they finished cooking, after it has been strained.

Veal Olives

Thin veal steaks
1 Egg yolk
Thin rasher of bacon
Breadcrumbs
Grated lemon peel
Chopped parsley
Butter
Salt and pepper
2 cups Consommé or gravy
1 teaspoon lemon pickle
Catsup
Anchovy paste
Cayenne flour

The meat should be beaten and flattened as for *escalopes;* trim it so that each small steak shall be of the same size and shape. Brush over with egg yolk. Lay a very thin rasher of bacon on top of each piece of veal; strew over a few breadcrumbs, a little lemon peel and chopped parsley. Tie each olive securely, then put them all in a baking pan, adding butter as for a joint, and seasoning with salt and pepper. Add to the Consommé or gravy, the lemon pickle, catsup, anchovy essence, and as much Cayenne as you wish. Dress all over lightly with flour and cook until brown, basting with the seasoned gravy. Strain gravy over the olives to serve.

Gateau Mille-Feuille

You can bake this yourself, but it is really much easier and altogether safer to buy a Mille-Feuille from any of the good *Pâtissiers* in town. They are sold as Napoleons.

MENU XIX

Crème de Riz

*   *   *

Darne de Saumon à la Daumont

*   *   *

Aiguillettes de Canard Bigarade

*   *   *

Fonds d'Artichauts Florentine

*   *   *

Pêches Melba

Just a small glass of a good Golden Sherry would be best immediately after the soup, but a much more generous allowance of a dry white wine would be expected to be served with the fish: there are so many to choose from that it is or should be easy to find just the wine that would please most if not all your guests: a white Bordeaux such as Château Laville Haut-Brion; a Chablis Premier Cru or a Meursault Charmes would probably be easier to buy than other white wines which are made in smaller quantities and not exported to nearly the same extent; such as Quincy, from the Upper Loire country, Bellet from Provence, Merlu Riesling from Yugoslavia, or Bataton Riesling from Hungary. With the Duck and the Artichauts one could hardly do better than choose one of the good Bred Burgundies, a Slos des Grandes Vignes of Nuits St. Georges, for example. And to finish with, just one glass—not quite as small as the first—of a sweeter wine, either a Sauternes such as a Château Rayne-Vigneau, or a Palatinate wines such as a Kallstadter Steinacker Riesling.

RECIPES

Crème de Riz

Wash, blanch and drain some rice, then cook it either in milk or chicken broth, adding salt, pepper, and some butter. When the rice is cooked and soft, push it through a fine sieve, return it sieved to the pot in which it was cooked, re-heat after adding to it as much fresh cream as will look and taste right.

Darne de Saumon à la Daumont

Poach a *Darne* (middle cut) of Salmon on a slow fire in an open pan in some dry white wine which must only just cover the whole of the fish; season with salt and pepper; add an onion and a carrot, sliced; also some twigs of parsley, half a leaf of bayleaf, and one piece of thyme. When the fish is cooked—but be sure you do not overcook it—dress it on a serving dish and garnish it with fish *Quennelles,* mushroom caps tossed in butter, soft roes floured and also tossed in butter; truffles and crayfish tails—if you can get them! The right sauce to serve is a *Sauce Normande.*

Aiguillettes de Canard Bigarade

Clean, singe, and truss a large duck. Put at the bottom of a large pan sufficient peeled and sliced onions and carrots to make a nicely padded cushion for the duck to sit on comfortably. Add some veal bones and trimmings if possible, also a small *bouquet garni,* pepper and salt, and some *bardes de lard* (thin strips of fresh pork skin). Cook on a gentle heat until the duck is done, then take it out of the pan, drain it and keep it warm in the oven.

Strain the gravy from the pan through a fine sieve; make a light *roux* with a little sifted flour and butter, and moisten it with some of the sieved gravy after you have skimmed all excess of fat. Cook gently for a few minutes and add the juice of a bitter orange.

Lift the *Aiguillettes* (thin slivers carved longways from both sides of the duck's breast); arrange them in the serving dish, pour over them the sauce, and serve hot.

Fonds D'artichauts Florentine

Trim, blanch and drain the required number of Artichoke bottoms; toss them in hot butter and season with salt and pepper. Pile up on each one a little creamed spinach, cover the spinach with some *Mornay* (cheese) Sauce, brown under a hot grill and serve hot.

Pêches Melba

Pêches Melba are ripe peaches which are skinned and served on a bed of vanilla ice, and covered with fresh raspberry *purée* or jam.

MENU XX

Turtle Soup

*   *   *

Soles au Chablis

*   *   *

Poulet en Cocotte Bordelaise

*   *   *

Salade de Saison

*   *   *

Omelette au Rhum

With the Turtle Soup a glass or two of a fine old Verdelho Madeira would be gratefully received, and since the soles are to be cooked in Chablis, it would be considerate to serve with them a Chablis Vaudésir, Grenouilles or Blanchot. With the Chicken to be cooked in the Bordeaux tradition, a Claret would also be expected as its partner, either a Château Rauzan-Gassies from the Médoc, a Château Haut-Bailly from the Graves de Bordeaux, or a Château Cheval Blanc, the finest Graves de St. Emilion. With the sweet Omelette there is no better choice than a lively Champagne.

RECIPES

Soles au Chablis

For four persons take four soles weighing about 7 oz. each. Wash and trim them, and break the backbone of each in the middle so that they will be flat. Butter a large fireproof dish and put into it four thin rounds of onions: on these lay the soles, placing them so that they will not touch each other. Add half a glass of Chablis, the liquid from a handful of mussels (which have been opened in a little hot wine), and enough water just to cover the fish. Cover with greased paper and cook for about 15 minutes in the oven.

The sauce:

Strain off the liquid from the soles and, placing them where they will be kept hot, reduce it to half its original volume. Thicken with a little flour and butter. Take the sauce off the fire after it has cooked for 8 minutes and add the yolks of 2 eggs diluted with a few drops of water. Beat well till thoroughly mixed. Put the sauce back on to a strong flame and let it just come to the boil, stirring all the time. Add the juice of a half a lemon and 3 ounces butter, a little at the time. Stir vigorously without letting the mixture come to the boil, until it has thickened.

Put the soles in a fireproof dish, cover them with sauce. Set the dish in another containing hot water and brown in a very hot oven. Serve at once.

(Recipe of C. H. Bergerand, Hôtel del E'Etoile, Chablis).

Poulet en Cocotte Bordelaise

Prepare the chicken as for roasting. Melt 3 tablespoons of butter in an earthenware or oven-glass cocotte, put in the bird and season with pepper and salt. Brown the bird on all sides evenly, then reduce heat and cover the cocotte. Meanwhile prepare some small new potatoes, button onions and artichoke bottoms—canned ones will do and they should be diced in another saucepan in hot butter, then add them and the diced artichokes to the cocotte where the chicken is cooking; let them cook together until the chicken is done, and serve it in the cocotte adding a few sprigs of parsley at the last moment to decorate it.

Omelette au Rhum

Make an omelette in the ordinary way and fold in it when ready to be served some warmed apricot jam; then pour over it some warmed rum, set it alight and serve it with some iced whipped cream, which is handed round in a sauce-boat.

MENU XXI

Consommé de volaille

*   *   *

Coquilles St. Jacques au Gratin

*   *   *

Boeuf à la Russe

*   *   *

Chou-marin Mornay

*   *   *

Glace Abricotine

There is no call for any wine to drink immediately after the light chicken broth. With the highly seasoned scallops a white wine of Arbois, in the Jura, or of Bandol, in Provence, should prove interesting and refreshing. With the Beef and the cheesed sea-kale one of the red wines of Chambolle-Musigny, either a Charmes, Bonnes Mares or Musigny, to name but three of Chambolle-Musigny's best vineyards. With the Apricot ice, a glass of Abricotine, one of Garnier's popular liqueurs, would be appropriate, or any of the many apricot liqueurs and cordials available.

RECIPES

Consommé de Volaille

Clean and truss a fowl and put it into a large pot with just enough water to cover it; add a slice or two of onion and a blade of mace; also salt and pepper; a carrot, a small leek, and a stick of celery, when available, should go in as they all help. Simmer gently until the fowl is thoroughly well done; take it out of the pot and strain the soup; let it get cold and skim off any fat that comes to the surface. Re-heat when wanted and add to the Consommé before serving a teaspoon of almonds which you should pound to a paste beforehand.

Coquilles St. Jacques au Gratin

Select bay scallops and cut them into cubes after boiling in salted water for a few minutes. Braise in white wine until tender, mix with chopped mushrooms which have first been tossed in hot butter; cover with breadcrumbs, a pat or two of butter, and brown in a hot oven or under the grill.

Boeuf à La Russe

Chop finely about 1 pound tender raw beef; season with salt, pepper, and a pinch of mixed herbs; mix with 2 tablespoons of uncooked rice and shape into small sausages. Parboil a small cabbage, detach leaves and remove hard stalks. Wrap each little sausage in a cabbage leaf; tie into neat shapes and place in a deep pan; cover them with a rather thin tomato sauce. Cook slowly for one hour, then strain in a little flour blended with cold water or stock. Season with lemon juice and serve hot.

Chou-Marin Mornay

Wash and trim the sea-kale and tie it up in a bundle; parboil it in salted boiling water for a very short time and drain; then put the sea-kale in a fireproof dish, cover it with a Sauce Mornay and bake in a hot oven till nicely browned.

Glace Abricotine

Peel and stone the apricots or open a can of apricots and drain fruit well. Boil some sugar and water, remove scum as it rises and put in the fruit; simmer until mushy and then let it get quite cold. Freeze 3 cups of thin cream for each cup of apricot pulp; add pulp, a pinch of salt and more or less sugar according to taste; also a dash of lemon juice; then freeze the lot and keep it in the refrigerator until wanted.

MENU XXII

Soupe à l'Oignon gratinée

*   *   *

Pompano à l'Angevine

*   *   *

Epaule d'agneau aux Navets

*   *   *

Salade de saison

*   *   *

Soufflè of chicken

To begin with, one might try and get a white wine somewhat out of the ordinary, a Rully or a Givry, for instance, little known white Burgandies which are quite nice, simple and straightforward wines; or else a white Seyssel from the Upper Rhône Valley, on the Savoie border. With the lamb and the chicken we might also try and get a red wine rather unusual such as a St. Nicholas de Bourgueuil, from Touraine. And with the fruit we ought to return to the traditional dessert wine, a Vintage Port bearing the name of one of the famous Port Shippers.

RECIPES

Soupe à L'oignon Gratinée

Peel 4 or 5 onions, cut them up finely. Heat a tablespoon of butter in a frying pan, and fry in it gently the chopped onions, and stir all the time until the onions are nicely browned. Stir in a tablespoon of flour; moisten with a little meat stock or hot water; then slip the whole contents of the frying pan into about a quart of good meat stock in a deep pan. Bring to the boil, then reduce heat and simmer for 20 to 30 minutes when the soup should be ready to serve. Pour it into as many individual soup bowls as there are guests; add 2 or 3 thin slices of French bread, dried in the oven, in each bowl; sprinkle with grated cheese, brown under the grill and serve very hot.

Pompano à L'angevine

Clean the required number of pompano thoroughly and slit side half-way down. Soak a cupful of breadcrumbs in half a cup of milk, adding a finely chopped onion, butter and a coarsely chopped hard boiled egg. Squeeze out any superflous milk and season with pepper and salt. Mix to a paste, add some lemon juice and use the mixture to stuff the fish, sewing the slit after the stuffing has been put in. Lay the prepared fish in a sheet of well oiled white paper. Place in an oven dish and cook for 45 minutes; then remove paper and serve with slices of lemon and fried parsley.

Epaule d'agneau

For this dish it is necessary first of all to ask the butcher to bone and roll the shoulder of lamb you have bought from him. Sprinkle the meat with salt, pepper and a pinch of ground ginger. Heat a couple tablespoons of butter in a pan and brown the meat in it, then cover it—only just—with stock, broth or plain water, if need be. Cook on a moderate heat allowing 15 minutes per pound. Then add about 2 pounds of small young turnips and a clove of garlic. Cover and go on cooking for a further 15 minutes per pound. Skim excess of fat and serve very hot.

Soufflé of Chicken

Remove all skin and gristle from a roast or boiled chicken and mince the meat finely; season with pepper and salt, pound in a mortar and press through a sieve. Add a little more pepper and salt and the well beaten yolks of 3 eggs which must be thoroughly well blended with the meat. Beat the egg whites until very stiff and lightly fold them into the chicken mixture. Pour all into a buttered soufflé mold, and cook in a moderately hot oven for 25 or 30 minutes, or until well risen and lightly browned on top, then serve at once.

MENU XXIII

Velouté de Crevettes

* * *

Rognons au Madère

* * *

Perdreau rôti sur Canapé

* * *

Artichauts à la Barigoule

* * *

Soufflé au Fromage

Fruits

With the Fish soup a glass of Amontillado Sherry will clear the gustatory buds of all fishiness so that we may appreciate to the full a fine Claret, such as a Clos Fourtet, which would partner very well the *Rognons* and lead the way for one of the really great red Burgundies with the partridge, either a Clos de Tart or a Château-Gris, one of the best and too little known wines of Nuits St. Georges. To end with, a Bual or a Malmsey Madeira would be rather nice.

RECIPES

Velouté de Crevettes

Make a good rich fish broth and thicken it slightly with a little rice flour (one tablespoon to 1 pint of liquid). Boil the shrimps, shell them, and pound them in a mortar until smooth; pass them through a wire sieve, put in the fish broth, and add the yolks of 4 eggs and 1 cup of cream to 1 quart of soup. Mix well, reheat and serve hot.

Rognons au Madère

Skin some lamb kidney, cut each one in halves and each half in 2 or 3 pieces according to size. Heat some butter in a saucepan, then put in it the pieces of kidneys and about the same number of pieces of peeled, washed and sliced mushrooms. Cook on a rather lively heat until all the water from the mushrooms has steamed away and the butter runs clear. Season with salt and pepper; sprinkle with a little flour, moisten with as much dry Sherry as you believe will be good for you and the kidneys; squeeze the juice of half a lemon over it all, sprinkle with chopped parsley and serve hot.

Perdreau Rôti Sur Canapé

A plump young partridge, not too fresh but by no means approaching the 'high' mark—about 4 days after being shot, if well shot and the weather not thundery—is best plainly roasted and with no other sauce than the butter with which it was basted when cooking mixed with the fat and the blood of the little bird which will have oozed from it in the cooking.

Pluck, draw and dress the Partridge in the same way as you would a chicken. Season with salt and pepper, Cover the breast with a thin rasher of fat bacon, and roast on a spit in front of a bright fire for 30 minutes, or in a moderate over for 25 minutes, basting frequently. Serve on a thick piece of buttered toast with straw potatoes and some watercress undressed.

Artichauts à la Barigoule

Small and tender *Artichauts* must be chosen for this dish. Put a tablespoon of olive oil in a pan; slice an onion and dice a couple of small carrots; put them in the pan as soon as the oil is really hot; then put the *Artichauts* on top of them, sitting up, leaves up. Season with pepper and salt; pour another tablespoon of olive oil over the *Artichauts*. Cover and cook gently, shaking the pan now and again to prevent 'sticking'. When onion and carrots begin to brown, add a glassful of dry white wine and go on cooking until this is reduced by half. Then add a clove of garlic and a spoonful or two of water or stock, and finish cooking. When the artichokes are done, squeeze the juice of a small lemon over them and serve hot.

MENU XXIV

Purée Compiegne

*   *   *

Homard à l'Américaine

*   *   *

Noisettes d'Agneau Beauharnais

*   *   *

Zucchini au gratin

*   *   *

Nectarines and Peaches au Sauternes

A Bâtard-Montrachet, one of the most attractive white Burgundies, would be a fine start and it could be followed by one of the great aristocrats of the Médoc, a Château Latour, for instance, which would partner admirably the lamb. With the fresh nectarines and peaches, peeled, cut in quarters, and served in a salad bowl with a little sugar and no other dressing than an iced Sauternes the best wine would be the best Sauterne there is, a Château d'Yquem.

RECIPES

Purée Compiègne

Put some white butter or Lima beans in a pan, cover them with cold water and bring to the boil very slowly; when the water begins to boil, remove all surface scum and put into the pan a couple of onions with cloves stuck in them, and 2 or 3 carrots cut in halves or quarters according to size; also a *bouquet garni* made up of a sprig of thyme, half a bay leaf, a clove of garlic and a stick or two of celery. Season with pepper and salt, cover the pan or pot and simmer till the beans are tender. Drain the beans but save the water in which they were cooked. Rub the beans through a sieve which will give you a *purée* of beans; put it back into the pan with as much of the cooking water required for half the quantity of soup you intend making; add the same quantity of milk as you did water; season with pepper and salt; stir well and bring to the boil again; then, just before serving, stir into the soup a handful of sorrel, shredded and cooked in butter.

Homard à L'americaine

Cut up the lobster meat into 4 or 5 pieces, setting aside the coral and the greenish liver. Put two tablespoons of butter in an earthenware pan; heat it and when it is hot put in the pieces of lobster and increase the heat; toss the lobster in the sizzling butter, and then add an onion (sliced), a carrot (sliced), a *bouquet garni,* and a few sticks of celery. Shake the saucepan vigorously so that the whole shall go on cooking together, then pour over it all a glass of good brandy set it alight and leave it to burn itself out. Now add 2 teaspoons of meat glaze, 1 tablespoon of fresh tomato *purée,* and a glass of white wine. Season well with pepper and salt. Keep hot in slow oven or on top of the stove. In another oven dish place a tablespoon of butter, set it on top of the stove and, when very hot, add the coral and the green part of the fish, blending all this well for a moment or two. Remove and pound the mixture in a mortar with another 2 tablespoons of butter. When ready to serve, arrange the pieces of lobster on a hot dish and keep hot. Mix the sauce in the first pan with the pounded mixture and pour this over the lobster, sprinkling some finely chopped parsley over it all.

Noisettes D'agneau Beauharnais

Small pieces of lean meat of lamb, cut roundwise, and taken from the forequarter or fillet, pan-fried in butter and dressed on fried pieces of bread; served with very small, whole artichoke bottoms filled with a Sauce Beauharnais. This is a mushroom sauce with plenty of chopped tarragon leaves on it.

Zucchini au Gratin

Peel some tender young Zucchini; cut into thick rounds of equal thickness and boil for 2 or 3 minutes in salted boiling water. Drain when tender but before they are soft. Brown the slices lightly in hot butter on both sides. Season and put in a gratin dish, cover with good Béchamel sauce, sprinkle with grated cheese, dot with pats of butter, brown under grill and serve in the gratin dish.

MENU XXV

Créme Montespan

*   *   *

Sweetbreads à l'ancienne

*   *   *

Guinea Fowl au Calvados

*   *   *

Salade russe

*   *   *

Fraises Chantilly

The first wine for this dinner might be one of the good but not really great Clarets, either a Château Lanessan or a Château Rouet, the first being one of the more attractive Bourgeois growths of the Médoc, and the other a rather stouter wine of the Fronsac region, and incidentally, Château Rouet is well worth a visit if only for the sake of the truly magnificent panorama view to be seen from the terrasse of the Château. With the Guinea fowl, we might have a really great Claret, a Château Mouton-Rothschild, for instance, or else switch over to Burgundy and serve a Bonnes Mares, the best vineyard of Morey St. Denis and one of the best of the adjoining parish of Chambolle-Musigny. With the Strawberries and Cream, Champagne would surely be welcome.

RECIPES

Purée Montespan

This is an Asparagus soup with tapioca added to give it more substance.

Sweetbreads à L'ancienne

Blanch one or two sets of sweetbreads in boiling water for a few minutes, then drain and put into cold water to harden a little. Drain again and put in a casserole with about 1½ cups of good bouillon or stock, salt, pepper, a couple of onions, and a branch or two of parsley. Work a little flour in some butter and add to the pan. Simmer it all for half an hour. Beat an egg or two thoroughly well with about ¼ cup of fresh cream, remove pan from the fire, blend the egg and cream mixture with the gravy in the pan. Sprinkle with a little finely chopped parsley, season with a dash of nutmeg and a squeeze of lemon. Strain the sauce from the pan and pour it over the sweetbreads. Sliced truffles, when available, add to the good looks and to the 'bouquet' of the dish.

Guinea Fowl au Calvados

Shred an onion and brown it in some sizzling butter. Add a little raw ham cut up in a dice, a handful of cooked rice and 3 small green apples (any of the more acid cooking applies will do) finely sliced. Moisten with a cup of chicken or veal stock. Season with pepper and salt, then cook the lot long enough for the rice to be soft but not stodgy.

Prepare a young and tender Guinea Fowl just as you would a chicken; fill it with the rice-cum-apple stuffing, and sew it up securely. Tie some bacon rashers over the breast of the bird which may be either braised on top of the stove in a casserole, or roasted on a spit in front of a brisk fire. When the bird will be done, pour some *Calvados* or Apple-Jack over it, set it alight and let it burn itself out. Serve with a rich cream sauce rather highly seasoned.

[*Editorial Note:* Rock Cornish games hens or squabs may replace Guinea Fowl.]

Salade Russe

This is a salad in which as many cold, cooked vegetables as may be available are mixed and served with a Mayonnaise sauce as dressing: garden peas, French beans, diced carrots and potatoes are *de rigueur,* but there are a number of other vegetables which may be introduced and welcome.

MENU XXVI

Consommé Nemours

*   *   *

Sole Normande

*   *   *

Filet de Boeuf Madère, Tomates Provençale

*   *   *

Pineapple Ice Cream

There is no need to serve any wine immediately after the consommé, and the first wine should come in with the fish, a white wine, of course, and one of the very best to partner a noble dish; the choice might be between Le Montrachet, a noble white Burgundy, or Schloss Johannisberger Fürst Metternichscher Cabinet Auslese, a noble Hock. *Noblesse oblige* and the red wine which is to follow, to partner the fillet of beef, will have to be also one or the great aristocrats of either Bordeaux or Burgundy, such as a Château Ausone or La Romanée Conti. Pineapple is very nice but it does not help any wine; its own flavor is too pungent to give any delicate wine a real chance. However, a glass of chilled Coulée de Sarrant or La Roche aux Moines, two of the best vineyards of the Coteaux de la Loire, south of Angers, would be a sweet and gracious finish to this meal.

RECIPES

Consommé Nemours

This is a chicken broth with a little tapioca to thicken it, a garnish of carrots, and a *Julienne* of truffles.

Sole Normande

1 large sole
1 pint fresh mussels
1 dozen oysters
½ pint shrimps
White wine
Salt and pepper
Butter
½ lb. mushrooms
Flour
½ cup thick cream
1 shallot

Have the sole filleted. Open the mussels over the fire, take them out of the shells and save their liquor. Open the oysters and carefully strain their liquor; keep it aside. Shell some fine shrimps, and keep aside the shells and heads. Place about 1 cupful of white wine with the same quantity of water in a small saucepan. Add the head and bones of the sole, the heads and shells of the shrimps, the liquor from the mussels and oysters, salt, pepper, the shallot, and the butter in which the sliced mushrooms have been gently cooked. Cook all this slowly for a half an hour, then strain through muslin. Re-heat and use to poach the fillets of sole until done—which will take from 10 to 12 minutes' slow cooking. Remove fillets and lay them in a buttered baking dish, longways. Mix 4 or 5 tablespoons flour with the same amount of heated butter, as when making an ordinary white sauce, moisten with the strained extract of fish and cook for 5 minutes gently, then add cream and see that the seasoning is as it should be. Pour this over the fillets of sole, decorating with mushrooms, shrimps, mussels and oysters, nicely arrange to form a border. Pass under the flame of a gas grill or in an oven to color surface slightly and serve in the cooking dish.

Filet de Boeuf Madère

> *Middle piece of a fillet of beef*
> *Butter*
> *Larding bacon*
> *Salt and pepper*
> *Sauce Madère*

Cut the larding bacon into thin strips and use them for
'larding' the fillet of beef with the special 'larding needle' made
for the purpose; trim, shape and tie up neatly the 'larded' meat;
and put it in a *very hot* oven so that the surface be quickly
browned. For underdone meat—which is best—allow from 15
to 20 minutes per pound. Baste well while cooking and, when
done, use the gravy as a foundation for the *Sauce Madère*.
Mushrooms and thin slices of truffle are the traditional garnish
of this dish which is served with a *Sauce Madère* handed round
separately, and *not* poured over the joint.

Tomates Provençale

> *1 lb. firm and even sliced tomatoes*
> *1 or 2 cloves of garlic*
> *5 or 6 shallots*
> *3 tablespoons breadcrumbs*
> *Chopped parsley*
> *Salt and pepper*
> *3 tablespoons olive oil*

Cut the tomatoes into halves. Finely chop together the shallots and the garlic. Crumble the stale white breadcrumbs finely
and chop the parsley. Now put the olive oil in a pan large
enough for the tomatoes to cook without touching each other.
When the oil is smoking, add the shallots and garlic, then the
tomatoes, cooking gently after pricking them with a fork to let

the water ooze out of them. When the oil is clear and the tomatoes have been cooked on both sides, add the breadcrumbs, browning them in the oil, and then sprinkle them with the parsley over the tomatoes. Season with salt and pepper. Serve hot.

Pineapple Ice-Cream

Crush 1 pound fresh pineapple and mix in one and a half pounds milk flavored with vanilla and ½ pound sugar. Strain and freeze.

MENU XXVII

Consommé Cyrano

*   *   *

Filets de Truite Vauclusienne

*   *   *

Rôti de Veau Bourgeoise

*   *   *

Aubergines gratinees

*   *   *

Pêche Condé

With the Consommé and the Vauclusienne Trout, both quite uncommon, a nice white wine which is also uncommon should be suitable, one of the Moselle wines from the Luxembourg vineyards, such as a Remicher, for instance. With the rest of the meal, however, a white wine with greater body and bouquet would be desirable, such as an Erbacher Marcobrunnen or Schloss Reinhartshausener, the famous Chateau and vineyard near Erbach-am-Rhein, the property of Prinz Friedrich Heinrich of Prussia.

RECIPES

Consommé Cyrano

This is a meat or chicken Consommé, made with the usual vegetables, but flavored with some duck *fumet* and garnished with *quenelles* of pounded and sieved duck meat.

Filets de Truite Vauclusienne

A rather large Trout filleted
White wine
Boiled crayfish
Fresh mushrooms
1 chopped truffle
Thick Béchamel sauce
Egg yolks
Lemon juice
Salt and cayenne
1 beaten egg
Fine brown breadcrumbs
Butter
Deep fat for frying

This is a somewhat sophisticated dish, and a very delicious one. Poach the fillets of trout in white wine, then drain them and cut them into triangular pieces. Boil the crayfish and shell them, crack the claws neatly and keep them aside. Cut up the meat from the crayfish tails into small dice, mix with chopped mushrooms, the truffle and sufficient thick Béchamel sauce to bind the mixture to a thick paste. The Béchamel has to be thickened with one or more egg yolks, and flavored with lemon juice, salt and cayenne to taste. Spread the mixture on each piece of fish, coating evenly and pressing flat with a palette knife. Dip each piece of fish thus prepared first of all into beaten egg, then into breadcrumbs; allow each piece to harden, then fry a golden brown in deep fat. Serve piled on one another, the corners of each triangle being ornamented with one of the tiny crayfish claws stuck into it at right angle.

Rôti de Veau Bourgeoise

Veal is much drier meat than either beef or mutton so that it is always best to cook it with some kind of fat. The 'bourgeoise method is 'larding' the joint, with a special larding needle, before roasting it. It is also important to remember that veal must be cooked very slowly and basted more than any other meat if it is to be tender. It is served with little button onions which have been cooked in butter, and small new carrots which are blanched and then tossed in butter and sprinkled over with chopped parsley.

Aubergines Gratineés

Slice some egg plant or aubergines as you would slice a cucumber and cook the thin slives in olive oil or butter till they are nearly black. Take them out of the pan and arrange them in thick rows in a shallow baking dish. Cover them with equal quantities of cream and tomato *purée;* sprinkle some breadcrumbs on top and dot about some pats of butter; bake in a moderate oven till browned.

Pèche Condé

Scald and peel whatever number of freestone peaches you may require; cut them in half, sugar them at once so that they do not brown. Fill up individual shallow footed glass dessert cups with some rich, sweet rice pudding, and place a half peach, inverted on the rice so that it looks like a golden dome topping the white rice. Pour over it 3 or 4 tablespoons of raspberry sauce.

MENU XXVIII

Potage Crécy

*   *   *

Coquilles of Cod

*   *   *

Salmis de Faisan, Céleriac fritters

*   *   *

Apple snow

One of the lighter white Burgundies, such as Pouill-Vinzelles, could be served first and followed by a fine red Burgundy such as a Beaune Gréves Enfant Jesus, or a Nuits St. Georges Les Vaucrains. A glass of dessert Sherry, Bristol Cream or a rich Oloroso might be welcome change for a last wine.

RECIPES

Potage Crécy

Wash and scrub 5 or 6 large carrots and simmer until tender in salted water. Peel, cut in two, longways, and remove the core. Rub the carrots through a sieve and reheat the water in which they were cooked; when it comes to the boil, put in a handful of rice, and then the mashed carrots. Simmer gently until the rice is soft but not mushy. Season with salt, pepper, and butter; add the beaten yolk of an egg and a little fresh cream, and serve hot.

Coquilles of Cod

Boil or steam the required quantity of fresh cod; let it get cold, then pick over carefully, removing skin and bones. Flake with a fork and mix with a thick white sauce made whilst the cod is cooking; season with pepper and salt and flavor with lemon juice. Place in scallop shells the mixture of sauced cod, surround with a border of mashed potatoes and garnish with some fresh mushrooms which have been sliced and tossed in butter. Sprinkle the fish with breadcrumbs, dot about some pats of butter, and brown in a quick oven.

Salmis de Faisan

2 young pheasants
1 or 2 truffles
1 carrot
1 sprig dried thyme
Salt and pepper
1 tablespoon flour
2 or 3 shallots
Bay leaf
1 cup red wine
2 cups good stock
Croûtons

Prepare the birds as for roasting and wrap them in rashers of fat bacon. Roast them and when done carve them into five pieces: 2 legs, 2 wings, 1 breast. Put these pieces and the gravy in a small casserole with the sliced truffles. Keep warm without any further cooking. In another saucepan, place the minced shallots, the thinly sliced carrot, the thyme, bay leaf, salt, freshly ground pepper, the wine, the stock, and last but by no means least the bodies of the two birds. Cook until contents of pan have been greatly reduced in volume, then add the flour, mixed with a little stock or water, and continue the gentle simmering for 10 minutes or so. Dish up the pieces of pheasant, surround with *Croûtons* and strain the sauce over the whole.

Céleriac Fritters

Cut into long 'matches', or dice some celeriac, the Continental species of celery cultivated for its thick turnip-like stembase, and not its stalks. Boil them in salted water until tender; drain, dry in a cloth, dip in batter, fry crisp in hot fat and serve with fried parsley.

Apple Snow

Wash and dry 3 large cooking apples; prick them in a few places and bake them in a moderately hot oven until they are soft. Remove the skin and rub the pulp through a sieve. Beat the white of one egg to a froth, adding ⅓ cup sugar, little by little, then add apple pulp and beat it all together until thoroughly well mixed, light and soft.

MENU XXIX

Oxtail soup

*　　*　　*

Quenelles de Brochet

*　　*　　*

Ragoût of Goose, Carottes aux fines herbes

*　　*　　*

Chocolate Soufflé

*　　*　　*

Fruit

This might well be an all white wine Dinner, with a glass of Montilla Sherry with the soup, for Sherry is a white wine by birth if not by color, being made from white grapes; then a white Graves, a Château Carbonnieux or Domaine de Chevalier Blanc, leading up to a finer and more fragrant Hock such as a Schloss Böckelheimer Riesling Spatlese from the Nahe Valley.

RECIPES

Oxtail Soup

Have an oxtail cut in 1-in. pieces at thin end and the large root pieces sawn into 4 portions of equal size. Clean and dice an onion, a small turnip, a stalk of celery, and a carrot. Soak the pieces of tail in boiling water for a few minutes, then drain, dry and fry them in butter with the cut-up vegetables. Season rather highly. Put oxtail and vegetables in some good, rich stock in a deep pan, cover, and simmer for 4 hours, skimming frequently. Skim off fat and drain. Serve with small pieces of the oxtail meat in the soup; also a small glassful of dry Sherry.

Quenelles de Brochet

Crush in mortar 2 pounds of pike and mix in 1 pint of cream. Season and make into balls with a couple of spoons. Cook in fish stock and white wine, half and half, but do not boil. Take fish out when cooked; reduce the wine stock, add some more cream, and reduce again; then add ¼ pound butter and garnish with mushrooms cooked in butter.

Ragoût of Goose

Cut up a gosling into serving pieces and brown them in very little butter as goose skin contains a great deal of fat. Cut up an onion and about 2 pounds of tart cooking (peeled) apples into thick slices and put them in the pan with the pieces of goose. Season with salt and pepper and a tiny pinch of cinnamon. Cover the pan tightly and cook gently until the pieces of goose are tender. Skim off excess of fat and serve hot on a bed of apples.

Carottes Fines Herbes

Wash, scrub and peel some young carrots. Drain them, slice them and toss them in a frying pan for a few moments in fresh butter; season with pepper and salt and sprinkle over them some finely chopped parsley and chervil mixed. Serve with the Goose Ragoût.

MENU XXX

Bortsch

*   *   *

Grilled Salmon Steaks

*   *   *

Roast Hare

*   *   *

Asperges vertes, sauce Maltaise

*   *   *

Abricots à la Condé

A small glass of a dry Amontillado Sherry with the Bortsch, and a couple of glasses of a fine Alsatian wine, a Traminer of Schlumberger's shipping, for instance, with the salmon would make a good beginning. With the hare, a highly flavored dish, one of the more robust red Burgundies would be best, not necessarily one of the most famous, but a Pommard, Dames de la Charité Curvée of the Hospices de Beaune, or a Volnay, Cuvée Général Muteau, another of the Hospices de Beaune wines. After such fare and wines we might find a Sauternes or any other sweet dessert wine rather dull, and Champagne would certainly be a better choice.

RECIPES

Bortsch

Make a rich *Pot-au-feu* with 2 pounds beef, 1 pound smoked bacon and a duck; also a *bouquet-garni,* a large onion with cloves stuck in it, a spoonful of vinegar, and a tumblerful of squeezed beet juice flavored with some caraway seeds. Season with pepper and salt. Fry lightly in goose fat a *julienne* of shredded or sliced beets, cabbage, white of leeks, celery roots and onions, and add it all to the pot as soon as the meat will be nearly done. When it is quite done, take the meat out, cut it up, add some crisp chipolata sausages, and serve immediately after the soup. Before serving the soup itself, add as much sour cream as you fancy. Heat again and taste again, seasoning with more pepper and salt if need be.

Grilled Salmon Steaks

Cut 1-inch thick steaks from the middle cut of a fairly large salmon; dust lightly with salt and a speck of cayenne. Grill under a hot grill with or without an oiled paper wrapping, and serve with a *Sauce Tartare*.

Sauce Tartare

Finely chopped parsley and tarragon
Salt and pepper
Red wine vinegar
2 or 3 coarsely chopped gherkins
French Dijon mustard
Dry white wine
Good stiff Mayonnaise sauce

Have all the ingredients ready to add to the Mayonnaise, together with about a teaspoonful of mustard. Thin to the required consistency with a little dry white wine and wine vinegar.

Roast Hare

1 hare
Butter
Thin rashers of bacon
Milk
1½ cups good stock
½ teaspoonful chopped shallot
Pinch of dried thyme
Butter
1 glass port wine
Flour
1 small onion, chopped
½ teasponful chopped parsley
Salt and pepper

A young hare, hung for a week, weather permitting, is best. Truss it and brush it over with melted butter. Cover the back with the rashers of bacon, tied or skewered on. Place in a baking tin with about a cupful of milk, and sprinkle with pepper and salt. Roast from 1½ to 2 hours, according to size and heat, basting frequently with the milk and a little more butter. The liver should have been removed to be boiled sperately, then drained and chopped finely. Melt a couple tablespoons of butter in a small saucepan, add the chopped liver, the parsley, the shallot, the onion and the thyme. Season it all well and fry it all gently for 10 minutes, then pound in a mortar and rub through a hair sieve. Take the butter that drained from this mixture, reheat it, add a good tablespoonful of flour, and cook together until it is a light brown color (*roux blond*), then add either stock or some of the milk used for basting the hare, stirring until it comes to the boil. Add the liver mixture, simmer 10 minutes longer, then add the port. When the hare is nearly done, remove the rashers of bacon, to brown the back, dredging it lightly with flour and basting frequently whilst it finishes browning. Remove strings, serve with the liver sauce and red currant jelly handed separately.

Sauce Maltaise

This sauce which is a change from the ordinary *Sauce Hollandaise* served with the green English Asparagus is a *Sauce Hollandaise* which has been both colored and flavored with the juice of some blood oranges.

Abricots à la Condé

Unmold upon a serving dish a border of boiled (sweetened) cold rice, flavored with a stick of vanilla. Set upon this border peeled apricots, whole or in halves, which have been boiled in a light syrup of sugar and water. Decorate with some candied fruits and pour over it all an apricot sauce flavored with kirsch.

INDEX